Joyful Moments Within Shadows

Molly Stocks

BookLeaf
Publishing

India | USA | UK

Made with ❤ on the BookLeaf Publishing Platform
www.bookleafpub.in
www.bookleafpub.com

Dedication

To all book lovers who finds worlds within pages and peace within words. These poems are for you may this book be your solace.

Preface

In the quiet moments of life, when shadows loom large and the weight of the world feels to heavy. The poetry has been my way to escape and be able to use my voice in a way that allows me to escape and giving me hope. The collection was born in the darkest of times, where each verse became a stepping stone towards light and joy. Within pages, I have woven together words and reflect resilience and capturing the fighting spirit of finding joy in despair. My journey through these poems shows the power of art, a reminder that even in the darkest times, joy will follow. I invite you to walk with me through the verses, to find solace and inspiration, and maybe a spark of joy in your darkest moment.

Acknowledgements

I am deeply grateful to all those who have supported me on this journey of bringing my poetry book to life. To my family, for their unwavering support and belief in my dreams,your love has been guiding light. A heartfelt thank you to my friends whose insights and feedback has enriched my work immeasurably. A special mention to my book club who has inspired me and supported me through this whole writing process and pushed me to do better. I would also like to express my love and appreciation for my boyfriend, whose support and understanding a strength throughout this whole process. Finally, to my readers, your enthusiasm and love for these poems gives me a purpose to each poem. Thank you all for being apart of this journey.

1. Breathe

I just wanted one more chance
One more dance
One more breath
One more walk
One more talk
One more thought
Tore in my heart
Beat into my soul
I choose silence
Silence in the pain
Seems like in vain
Not letting it stain
Just breathe

2. My Star

Lie in the breeze
Look at that Tree
Feel so Free
Feel the breeze
Feel alive
Two Doves
Two Loves
Tore into my heart
Stole from my heart
Keep it safe
Locked in my heart
There is not enough time
To keep you mine
Keep hope safe
In this sacred place
Let the music flow
Meet in the peace
Death took
While I stand
Still lie on the land

hands letting you go
On all the low
You fly high
My star

3. What a waste of time

Wasting time on you
What a waste of dime
You're Lucky
You got time
Leave you in read
Rather read my book
My bookcase calling
Flowers in my vase
Your lies
Can die
I know the truth
Bow to the truth
Books are better
Than your looks
No wasting my time

4. My Fantasy

Hook you in my book
Fantasy living in my head
No reality
My sanity is fictional
Living in a fantasy
Sounds fancy
Love calls
Love falls
Keeps you craving
Saving the world
Braving the next book

5. Head over heart

Missing you
Loving you
The hugging
It's bugging
Head hurting
Lurking in my heart
Summer of tarts
Summer of love
Flying like a dove
Kissing you
Glistening soul
Toll of love
No cost
Even when your lost
Soft love

6. Music to my soul

music sings to my soul
the rock that keeps me in place
been my firm foundation
the shadows in the dark
keeping me in the light
burning sunlight in my darkness
the peace that stays with me
the melody to sway to
the calmness in my storm
the lameness of being me didn't matter
as the calling comes to me
my heart being torn
the music stitching my heart
keeping it together
the wind following the melody

7. love is for the poets

Love is for the poets
The writers know heartbreak
To leak information into our hearts
The fictional worlds scream our names
It's not for the lame
We call for our story to be told
Not to be dolled
Not to be claimed for our looks
So we go to our books

8. no cure

In the depths of longing,
Where hope meets pain
A journey unfolds with a heavy heart to bear
No cure in sight
Dreams still longing
To their calling
In the search of answers don't fall
Through trials and tears we do our best
Each sunrise brings a new day to cope,
As we love our hope.

9. Silent Pain

In the silence of the body's hidden pain
A battle rages, unseen, yet deeply felt.
A name whispered in strain
Where strength and resilience quietly dwelt.

Each a day a testament to courage untold,
As warriors rise with grace through the ache.
In the shadows, stories of bravery unfold.

Amidst the struggle, hope's gentle embrace,
A reminder of the power within.
Turning whispers of pain into voices that win.

To those who fight this silent fight,
May your journey be met with
Understanding and care.
For in your strength shines a brilliant light,
A beacon of hope that will always be there.

10. This is love

In the quiet whisper of the night,
Your laughter dances, a soft, sweet light.
In your embrace i have found my place
As our hearts race.

With every glance, the worlds fades away,
In your eyes, the dawn of a new day.
Your love is a melody and so pure
In the chaos I found my heart's cure.

Through storms we wander, through the skies
The star shine so brightly
Looking at your light
With you by my side, the stars align.

11. Comedy is my escape

In a world of chaos
I lie low and hide in laughter
Sparking joy with jokes
Even when feeling low
They flow out of me
With silly punchlines to embrace
Comedy is my escape
My happy place

I dive into jokes like a sponge in the sea
Where laughter fills the room and i can just be
With witty quips and a wink of the eye
Life heavy burdens begin to let me be.

12. Lost in thoughts

You running through my mind
The tide flowing through my veins
In a quiet of a room
Where everything slows
A world inside, where dreams can soar,
In a calm of night, we explore

Walking through paths of what might be,
In the wide ocean of memory spree.
Pictures swirl, like shadows that lay,
In this place where reality fades away.

13. My Muse

In the quiet corner of my mind, you dwell,
A spark of inspiration, casting a spell.
The thoughts i want to tell,
My muse, my guide, in all that I pursue.

In your presence, words flow like a stream,
It's like being in a vivid dream.
I dream what this could all mean.

Through the shadows of doubt, you light the way,
A hope in my darkest day.
With every stroke of pen, I find,
The essence of you, have you in my mind.

14. Best friend Loyalty

In moments of joy, you share my delight,
In times of trouble, you're my guiding light.
With unwavering loyalty, you hold my hand,
Together we face storms,
Together we stand.

Through secrets told in the dead of night,
We trust and everything feels right.
The calm in the storm,
In the warmth of your friendship,
My heart is reborn.

Form in the realm of besties,
Loyalty reigns,
A bond unbroken,
through losses and gains.
In the book of life,
On every page,
Your friendship is a treasure that will never age.

15. Stars

Whispering tales of ages past,
The stars that shine forever to last.
Guiding sailors on the sea
In their wisdom we find our peace.

Each star a story,
In the cosmic dance,
In the presence, our souls abide
A wonder of galaxies vast and wide.
For in the stars, we see our place,
A reminder of the infinite above.
We find hope and love.

16. Beating through life

In the city's heartbeat, a siren wails,
A call to action, through streets and trails
A lifeline in the chaos.

Through the night, it lights flash bright,
A lake of memories.
In its wake, urgency and care,
A promise of help,
Is always there.

17. Unexpected Joys

In the routine of life, a surprise unfolds,
Little moments of joy,
More precious of gold.
A smile from a friend,
Talking to a stranger,
In these unexpected joys,
Our hearts mend.
A sunny rain on a sunny day,
A rainbow appears on a gray day.
In the simple pleasure of life,
The soul finds ease.

18. Life's punchlines

Lifes a journey, with twists and turns
Life stings and burns.
With humour and knowledge, it throws its lines,
In the punchlines of life, wisdom shines.

A stumble on the path,
In a great race, moments are rare.
With laughter to share.
In the irony of fate,
We find our grace,
In the punchlines, life's truth we embrace.

19. Absurdity of life

Cats in hats, and rain from the sun,
Life little quirks, a web spun.
In the jumble of events,
In absurdity, trouble lies.
The amount of time we try
We tie knots in life.

In their mystery, stories are told.
For life riddles unfolds,
In the absurdity, we dine
So raise a glass to the absurdity of life.

20. Bumblebee

In the garden bloom,
A bumblebee flies.
A tiny traveler on a flower hunt
Confronting its fears,
In every petal it finds rest.

Through the meadows and fields it roams,
It finds it home in the heart of the flower.
A humble creature with a role
In the dance of life, it plays a soul.

21. Reading into life

In the pages of life,
Each chapter is a mystery, waiting to be told.
Each has its role
In the book of existence, we find our soul

So turn each page,
In the novel of life,
Wisdom lies.
The truth we dare to find,
Read inbetween the lines
Letting the stories inspire
Who we are.

www.ingramcontent.com/pod-product-compliance
Lightning Source LLC
La Vergne TN
LVHW051248200726
843510LV00011B/1745